# The B
# CARDI JOKES

Collected by

Brian John

Greencroft Books
Trefelin, Cilgwyn, Newport,
Pembs SA42 OQN

1995
Reprinted 1997

The people of Ceredigion are still laughing at themselves, and jokes about the "Crafty Cardi" have become just as popular in Wales as the jokes about the tight-fisted Aberdonians in Scotland or the stupid Kerrymen in Ireland. By listening in to local raconteurs and sifting through my "joke mail" over the last year or so I have been surprised at the number of Cardi jokes still doing the rounds in English. Goodness knows how many more must be in common circulation in Welsh! I am sworn to secrecy as to my sources, but I can reveal that very few of the jokes in this book have come from the "foreigners" who live in Haverfordwest or Carmarthen. Most of the jokes actually seem to come from within Ceredigion. This means that the good people of the old county actually enjoy a good laugh at their own expense or the expense of their neighbours. This is very healthy. In the same way all the best Irish jokes actually come from inside Ireland.

The Crafty Cardi of all the stories is extremely tight-fisted, but also rather smart, and when it comes to a battle of wits he always comes out on top. So those who tell Cardi tales are having a bit of fun at the expense of the Cardis but also expressing more than a passing admiration for their quick wits and their awareness of human frailty. Long may the Cardi joke survive and flourish!

I have to acknowledge the help of many friends in putting together this collection of anecdotes. I have uncovered useful material in assorted publications by Trevor Fishlock, Christie Davies, Bob Phillips, John Aye, DB Knox, John Edwards and Murray Watts, and they would all agree that their published jokes are probably as old as the hills. Some of the jokes in this collection have never, so far as I know, appeared in print before. I claim no copyright in them, and will be only too happy for them to be used by others in whatever form they wish.

Copyright © Brian S. John 1995, 1997

Typesetting: Brian John

Printing: Haven Colourprint, Pembroke Dock

Design: Brian John using Claris Works software on Apple Mac LC475 computer

Illustrations: from Victorian children's comics and illustrated journals

# Greencroft Books, Trefelin, Cilgwyn, Newport, Pembs SA42 OQN     Tel: 01239 - 820470

# ISBN 0 905559 70 3

## Tragedy in Penparc

A tourist was speeding through Penparc on his way to Cardigan when he ran over Del Ifans' chicken and killed it stone dead. Stricken with remorse, the motorist picked up the dead bird and took it to the village shop, where he asked who the owner might be. "Oh yes, that will be belonging to Del Ifans," said the shopkeeper. So the motorist went to Del's house and admitted his crime.

"I am very sorry about your chicken, sir," said the tourist. "It ran out just in front of me and there was nothing I could do. If I give you £5 will that be all right?"

"Oh dear me." said Del, when he had recovered from the shock. "That was a very special hen. Better make it £10. You see, I has a cockerel that was very attached to that hen, and I am greatly afeared that when he finds out that she's dead the shock might kill him as well."

## Using the Media

Dewi Jones was very angry, having been badly treated by a well-known Cardigan grocer. So he placed an advert in the "Tivyside Advertiser" which read: "Yesterday I bought 4 lb of demerara sugar from a Cardigan grocer. When I came to use it I found that the sugar was mixed with about a pound of sand. If the shopkeeper in question doesn't send me a pound of clean sugar at once, I shall publish his name in next week's paper." Next day it was impossible to get up to Mr Jones' door owing to the throng of errand boys from every single grocer in town, all delivering 1 lb bags of demerara sugar.

## Enough for the Time Being

The representative from the local chicken farmer's cooperative was doing his rounds, and called in to Williams Grocer, one of his regular customers in Cardigan.

"Good day to you, Mr Williams bach." he said. "Will you be needing any new-laid eggs today?"

"Not today, thank you," replied Mr Williams. "This week has been a bit quiet with us, and we already have enough new-laid eggs in the back room to last us for a month."

## A Cardi Loan

"Wil, my good friend, I am having a few cash-flow problems just now. You couldn't lend me twenty quid, by any chance?"

"Oh, all right. On condition that you pays me back within the month."

"Most kind of you, to be sure. Tell you what. Just let me have ten pounds now, which will be enough to keep me going. Then I will owe you ten pounds and you will still owe me ten pounds. Shall we call it quits?"

## Leaving Cheaply

A Cardi was beaten in a business deal by a merchant from Haverfordwest, and such was the blow to his pride that he thought life was no longer worth living. So he went into Jones Chemist and asked for five shillings worth of arsenic. Somewhat concerned about the wild look in the Cardi's face, the chemist asked "And what would you be wanting it for, Mr Williams?" Without a moment's hesitation the Cardi replied "Half a crown, Mr Jones bach, and not a penny more."

## An Act of Faith

Caradoc Cueball was totally bald, and suddenly began to feel self-conscious about it when he fell in love with the ravishing Myfanwy. Determined to improve his image, and planning an intensive wooing campaign, he went into Jones Chemist one day and asked for a bottle of hair restorer. "I have just the thing," said Mr Jones. "This is a little preparation of our own, made from exotic herbs and spices imported from the gorilla jungles of South America.   One bottle costs  ninepence — expensive it may be,  but it is very efficacious indeed.   I can absolutely guarantee that within three weeks  of daily applications,  you will have a fine thick head of hair."

"Duw Duw, there's nice," replied Caradoc. "I will take a bottle if you please.  And while you are about it, please to wrap me up a brush and comb and a nice big pot of Brylcreem."

## A Nice Profit Margin

Tomos and Wynford were rough characters, reputed to be of gypsy extraction, who were frequently seen up and down the Teifi Valley selling brushes and other odds and ends.  One day they met up in Lampeter.  Tomos was upset.  "I am most offended," he said.  "I  called at a farm the other day and tried to sell the farmer's wife one of my brushes for two bob.  She said you had called a few days before and sold her one for a shilling.  How on earth can you sell them cheaper than me when I pinch my wood and my bristles, and then work on making the brushes at a devil of a speed?"

"No problem, old friend," replied Wynford.  "I pinch my brushes ready made, mostly from your shed when you are away pinching wood and bristles."

## Kindness Itself

An angry customer came storming into the grocery shop on the main street in Aberaeron.  "Look here," he remonstrated, "I bought a dozen oranges here this morning, and when I got home I found that there were only eleven."

"Oh yes indeed," said the shopkeeper.  "I remember it well.  About half past ten it was.  You did indeed buy a dozen oranges, but when I came to put them in a bag for you I found that one of them was rotten.  So, since in this establishment we pride ourselves on the service we provide to our esteemed customers, I threw it away for you."

## Dealing with Trouble

A small boy came into Hughes Grocer's shop in Llandysul and said to Mr Hughes: "Please sir, mother wants a pound of Welsh salted butter exactly the same as what she had with you last week. If it isn't exactly the same I am not to have it with you."

"Well, that's splendid," beamed the shopkeeper. "It's very pleasing to find a customer who is so delighted with the quality of my produce."

"Please to wrap it up then for me, Mr Hughes," said the boy. "It is very important, you see. A lot of father's relations are coming to tea today, and mother doesn't want them to come again."


## Just Checking

An old farmer from Llechryd was settling into the dentists chair in Trevor Griffiths' Dental Surgery in Cardigan. On being informed that he needed to have several teeth taken out, and that it would be advisable to have a general anaesthetic, the old farmer immediately took out his wallet and started counting through his pound notes.

"Don't you worry, Mr Pugh," said the dentist. "There is no need to pay me in advance. In fact, your treatment is on the National Health Service."

"I know that, dentist bach," replied the old man. "I'm just bein' careful with me money, and checkin' me worldly possessions afore ye sends me off to sleep with that there laughin' gas. I hopes to God my five quid will still be there when I comes to my senses again."

And before Mr Griffiths regained his composure the old man continued: "Now then, dentist bach, if I wakes up after all that laughin' in such a good mood that I tries to give me five quid away, please to stop me on the grounds that I has temporarily taken leave of me senses."


## Give unto the Lord — but not yet

Two old men belonged to the congregation of the Baptist Chapel in Cardigan. One Sunday morning they met after the morning service, and one said to the other: "Duw Duw, Albert, the state of the local economics is in good hands with the younger generation."

"Indeed? And what makes you say that, George?"

"Didn't you see young Morris Siop in chapel this morning?   Sitting right behind him, I was.  With his young son, he was.  Just before the collection he pinched him, and when the boy  started to cry he had to take him out.  Saved him a couple of bob, that's for sure."


## The  Crafty  Cardi

Once upon a time there was a wealthy farmer from Pembrokeshire who had three special friends.  One of them came from Carmarthen; another from Haverfordwest; and the third from Cardigan.  When the farmer died, his will stated that all his worldly possessions were to be shared equally between his three friends.  But there were two conditions.  Each friend had to be present at his funeral, and as a parting gesture each one had to place a gift of £100 in his cold hands as he lay in his open coffin before burial.

And so the morning of the funeral came.  The three friends visited the farmer's house and, each in turn, they went into the room where the open coffin lay.  The old farmer was laid out in style, dressed in his best suit and with a stiff starched collar. The Pembrokeshire man went in first, paid his last respects, and placed one hundred crisp pound notes in the dead man's hands.  Then the Carmarthen man did the same.  Finally  Evans, the Cardigan man, went in.  He took his wallet from his pocket, and discovered that it contained not even a halfpenny.  He felt in his jacket pockets and trouser pockets, and fared no better.  "Nevermind though," he said to himself.  "The old man will not be without his due."

And he took a cheque book from his waistcoat and carefully wrote out a cheque for £300.  Taking the two hundred pound notes from the coffin as change, he placed the cheque in the dead man's hand.  Then he replaced the lid on the coffin and went out of the room with a clear conscience, a bulging wallet, and an angelic smile on his face.


## The  Even  Craftier  Cardi

Shortly after the visit of the Crafty Cardi to the room where the coffin lay, another gentleman came in.  He had been asked by the deceased man's family to be one of the bearers at the funeral, and he also happened to come from Cardigan.  Being a careful Cardi, he thought he'd better check that all was well  in the coffin; and it occurred to him that he'd better have a quick rummage through the dead man's pockets just in case anything had been left there by accident.

On opening the coffin lid,  the gentleman was greatly surprised to find a cheque in the dead man's hands.  He prised it loose, opened it out, and was  delighted  to see the words "Pay the bearer £300", followed by the signature of one of the old farmer's friends.

"Duw Duw, there's nice of old Evans ," he said to himself. "Not often that people recognises the value of a good bearer. This little piece of paper must be for me." Then he replaced the coffin lid, screwed it down tight, and said not a word to anybody.

On the day after the funeral he went to the bank in Cardigan and cashed the cheque. When he found out, old Evans was not amused, for instead of being £200 richer, he was now £100 poorer than he had been before the funeral.

## Using the System

Two penniless men met in Haverfordwest. One of them was an unemployed farm worker from Cardigan, and the other was a Scot from Aberdeen. Both were in Pembrokeshire in the hope of finding jobs on the construction of the Esso Refinery. They were both thirsty and miserable, but then the Scot had an idea for getting a free drink. "There is a barmaid in the Milford Arms who likes to be chatted up," he said. "She also has a bad memory, and after a while she can't remember whether you've paid or not. Let's see if we can pull it off. I'll try first."

So they went into the Milford Arms, and the Cardi sat in the corner while the Scot duly got his free drink. Now it was the Cardi's turn to try, and he went up to the bar to order his pint. Soon he was engaged in deep conversation, telling the girl all about life in Cardiganshire. After ten minutes of animated discussion, he drained his glass and said: "Well, it's been nice talking to you, Susan. But now I must be off to meet a business colleague. What about my change?"

## The Cardi Visitor

Caleb Owen of Cardigan went off to visit his cousin in Cardiff. He had a wonderful time, for Cousin George treated him remarkably well. He drank well, ate well, was taken round to see the sights of the city, and even got a free ticket to a rugby international at the Arms Park. He overstayed his welcome by a week, and at last realised that his host was getting weary of his company. When George had taken him to the right platform on Cardiff station for the journey home, he said: "Cousin George bach, there's good you have been to me. I have ate well and drank well, and the match was wonderful. Indeed I don't know how to thank you, but I'll send you a hen now then, when it comes close to Christmas."

"Why, that's most kind of you, Caleb," said George. "I shall look forward to that." And he waved him goodbye.

About a year later the two cousins met up again at a family funeral. "Good day, Caleb," said George. "I thought you were going to send me a hen for Christmas?"

"So I was, Cousin George bach," replied Caleb. "But it never died."

# The Cardigan Death Test

Jeremiah Pugh was a respected councillor in Cardigan. He fell ill, and one evening a new GP from the local Health Centre received a call from his wife. "Please to call round, doctor bach," she said. "I think my beloved Jeremiah has just departed this life."

The doctor arrived within a few minutes, and started an examination of the body. "What are you doing, doctor bach?" asked Mrs Pugh. "Well now," replied the new GP, "I have to carry out these little tests just to make sure that your dear husband really has passed away."

"Oh, you needn't bother with all that," said the grieving wife. You're new around these parts, I suppose. All you need is a silver half-crown."

"And what on earth would I do with a silver half-crown, Mrs Pugh?"

"Just put in in the palm of his right hand, doctor bach. If his fingers don't close up to grasp it within a minute, the Good Lord have surely took him to Himself. We do say in Cardigan town that when the right hand have gone, bein' the money hand, there's no more point in stayin' alive anyway."

# The Crafty Cardi Goes to Town

A wealthy Cardigan merchant was travelling to London by train in the first class compartment. At first he was alone in the carriage, but at Whitland a Pembrokeshire man got in, and later another businessman joined them at Carmarthen station. As the journey went on the three got to talking about their great wealth and successful businesses. The conversation lapsed, and the three men settled into reading their newspapers. Then, as if to reinforce his boasts, the Pembrokeshire man put down his copy of "The News Chronicle". He ostentatiously took out a cigarette, lifted a pound note out of his wallet, ignited it with a match, and then lit his cigarette with it. A little later, not to be out-done, the Carmarthenshire man set aside his copy of "The Times". He extracted a splendid cigar from his gold cigar case, took out a five pound note, set it alight with a match, and applied it to his cigar.

A long time passed, with the three passengers apparently engrossed in their newspapers. Nobody said a word. At last the Cardiganshire man put down his newspaper. He rummaged in his pocket and took out a long briar pipe. Then, with no great haste, he packed it carefully with the finest tobacco. This task having been completed, and with his two travelling companions peeping over the tops of their newspapers, he slowly reached into his inside pocket. He took out his cheque book and, very deliberately, wrote out a cheque, saying quietly to himself "Pay the bearer one hundred pounds." Then he slowly put away the cheque book, put a match to the cheque, and used it to light his pipe. That having been done, he puffed away contentedly in a cloud of smoke all the way to London, totally absorbed in his copy of "The Tivyside Advertiser".

# Flexible Response

A benevolent old lady was walking past the Guildhall in Cardigan when she observed a beggar sitting on the steps with a sign next to him which said "Lame - local man, wife and six children to support." She stopped and looked with compassion on the poor man, and then placed a penny in his outstretched hand. "My poor fellow," she said, "here is a coin for you. Goodness me, it must be terrible to be lame. But I think it would be even worse to be blind." "Yer right, lady," agreed the beggar. "When I was blind I was always gettin' buttons and washers in me collectin' box!"

# Griff and the Match

Griff Morgan was a Cardigan man who travelled quite frequently on the "Cardi Bach" train between Cardigan and Whitland. One day he was settled happily into his corner seat, smoking his pipe as the train puffed its way towards Crymych. He got into conversation with a fellow passenger, and in due course the stranger took out his own pipe and started to fumble about in his pockets. Clearly he was searching for something.

"Dear me," he exclaimed, "I appear to have come out today without my matches. Can you oblige?"

Griff took a match out of his matchbox and handed it over. The fumbling continued, with the stranger making a great show of hunting through his pockets one by one. While all this was going on, Griff continued to smoke his pipe contentedly. At last the stranger spoke again. "This is really most annoying," he said. "I seem to have left my pouch of tobacco at home."

"Ah well," replied Griff. "You'd better be givin' me the match back, as you'll not be havin' any use for it now."

## A Stout Defence

A Cardigan man was travelling on the road to Narberth when he was leapt upon by three highwaymen. He put up a ferocious struggle but at long last the villains managed to pin him to the ground. On going through his pockets they found nothing but a bent six-penny piece. Surprised that the man had put up such a struggle in defence of such a small coin, one highwayman said to the others: "A must be a Cardi. And if a'd had a shillin' piece in 'is pocket a'd have surely killed the three of us!"

## Helping the War Effort

In the Second World War the good people of Cardigan were encouraged - like other citizens throughout the land - to put their money into War Savings. One day as Dai was coming out of the Post Office he met the local minister. "Good day to you, Dai," said the reverend gentleman. "I see you have been laying up treasure on earth, and at the same time helping the war effort."

"No, no, reverend bach," replied Dai. "I always comes into the Post Office on a Thursday, to fill up me fountain pen."


## Davy's Treasure

Davy Diamond was a labourer with a Cardigan building firm. He went up to Cardiff with the local rugby club to watch the Wales-England international match, and while he was there he did a bit of shopping. When he came back he showed all his friends at work a fine pair of gold cufflinks with large "diamonds" mounted on them. He wore them with pride every Sunday to chapel, and they were looked on with envy by family and friends. He treated with contempt any suggestion that they were not made with 18 carat gold and authentic diamonds. At last the foreman on the building site asked Davy, in strictest confidence, if the cuff-links from Cardiff had real diamonds on them.

"Course they have!" said Davy. "And if they ain't real diamonds some blighter have done me out of two bob!"


## No Liver Today

A Cardigan gentleman used to spend a penny a day on liver for his cat. One day he popped his head round the door of the butcher's shop and said:

"Don't you bother to send the liver round today, Billy. The cat have caught a mouse."


## A Ha'penny for Luck

Tomos, a young man from Cardigan, well brought up and thrifty with it, was intent upon making his way in the world. He applied for a job in London, and was invited for an interview. He became very apprehensive at the prospect of such a long journey, for he had not previously been further afield than Carmarthen. On confessing his fears to a friend, the friend said: "Don't worry. I heard from an old gypsy once that on a long journey by train you will get good luck if you throw a halfpenny out of the window every time you cross a river on the way."

Encouraged by this, Tomos went off to London, first on the Cardi Bach through Crymych and then on the GWR to London. When he returned he met his friend in the street, and was asked how he had got on with the good luck recipe.

"Not too bad indeed," replied the traveller. "I got on well enough crossing the Towy in Carmarthen and the Loughor at Neath, but when I got to the Taff at Cardiff the string got caffled up in the girders of the bridge, and I lost my ha'penny."


## The Religious Cardi

Mr Jones Generous was a religious Cardi gentleman who liked to watch his pennies, and think beautiful thoughts. One Sunday morning in chapel singing rousing hymns, he carelessly put a half crown on the collection plate, thinking it was a penny. Too late, he realised his mistake as the surprised sidesman nodded his approval and smiled a beatific smile. After that, the old gentleman only pretended to put money on the collection plate for the next thirty Sundays, till he was quits with God. From then on he examined his pennies very carefully before giving them to the Lord.

After some years Mr Jones stopped going to chapel because he was asked, once too often. to contribute to the Missionary Society. For the last twenty years of his life he made it his habit to listen to the Sunday morning service on the radio. He would settle down in his armchair and turn up the volume. He would sing lustily during the hymns and close his eyes devoutly during the prayers. When the collection was announced he would turn off the radio, and after a suitable time had elapsed he would turn it on again to continue with his devotions.

When at last he died the minister announced to the congregation: "Dear brothers and sisters, you will be moved to hear of the death of Mr Jones. His generosity was legendary. The funeral will be held in the chapel at 10 o'clock on Tuesday. I shall make a funeral address for the occasion, and the man himself will be here, for the first time in twenty years."


## The Missing Threepenny Piece

A Cardigan man was once seen in a local hostelry, frantically turning out his pockets and with a distraught expression on his face. "What's the trouble, Sion?" asked a friend.

"I've lost a threepenny bit and I've searched every pocket but one."

"Why don't you look in the last pocket, then?" he was asked.

"I'm scared to death, man," replied Sion. "For if it's not there the shock will surely be the finish of me!"

## Cardi Epistle

Letter from a Cardi written during a visit to London:

*"Dear Mam, There's a grand time I'm having here. The restaurants are especial good, and if I sits at a table where somebody have just finished I often finds a couple of bob under the plate! Mind you keep my cold rice pudding from Sunday. See you Friday off the Cardi Bach.*

*PS If there is no stamp on the envelope it have fell off in the post."*

## After all that Trouble

After the death of his wife Thomas Jones of Capel Dewi sent in an elaborate insurance claim under his fire policy, including the following: "Wife went up in smoke, £1000."

The insurance company rejected the claim, and the agent called round to give the reasons. Patiently he explained that the policy was strictly a property insurance and did not cover members of the family.

Mr Jones was greatly aggrieved at this. "Now you tell me!" he remonstrated in a loud voice. "After I have gone and paid out £50 to have Mary Jane cremated!"

## Sorting out the Problem

J.J. Morris the Cardigan Auctioneer was not too well, and for several days he went around town feeling very sorry for himself. He went to several of the local doctors to see if he could get the problem diagnosed, but got a different story from each of them. This did nothing for his peace of mind, and he became more and more depressed. A few days later he met his old friend Harold in the Guildhall in Cardigan, and mentioned his medical problem to him.

"Don't you worry, JJ bach," said Harold. "I have a friend in Cardiff who is better than those blokes on Harley Street. He can take a look at you, and what with all these scientific techniques he will have your trouble sorted out in no time at all."

"Sounds as if that might be a good idea," mused the auctioneer. "How much will it cost?"

"Normally fifty guineas, but for you I can probably arrange things for a price of twenty-five."

"Twenty-five guineas!" exclaimed Mr Morris. "Good Lord! I've already got a better price than that from Jones Undertaker!"

## Value for Money

A Cardi farm worker travelled up to Cardiff and decided to try out the services provided in a barber's shop in Westgate Street. "Please to tell me the price of a haircut," he said. "Eightpence old-fashioned, and ninepence posh, with Brylcreem," replied the barber.

"And how much for a shave?"

"Very good value at threepence."

"That's all right then," said the Cardi. "Please to give me a shaved head."

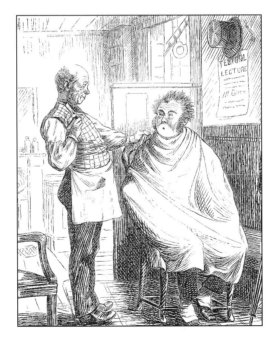

## Made to Last

David Parry had just died, and his wife had the sad task of organizing things for the funeral. She ordered a coffin from Billy Box and then went down the street to Jones Draper to get a shroud. "Good morning, Mrs Parry bach," said Mr Jones. "There's sad I am to hear your news. Bad business indeed."

"Thank you, Mr Jones bach," said Mrs Parry. "Grateful I am for your condolences. Now then, I have come to get a shroud for the dear departed. What will it cost me?"

"Seven and sixpence. Top quality - guaranteed to last a lifetime."

"Seven and six! But, Mr Jones bach, I can get one for five bob at Jenkins Siop Fach."

"That may be," said Mr Jones haughtily, "but you gets what you pays for in this world. I have some experience of Mr Jenkins' shrouds, and you can take it from me, Mrs Parry bach, that if you gets one from him the corpse will have his knees through it in a week."

## The Smell of Welsh Cakes

Harold and Mabel lived in a little cottage on one of the back streets of Aberystwyth. The cottage was immaculate, for Mabel was a fierce and tidy woman who liked to see everything in its place. She worked to a strict daily schedule, and was considerably inconvenienced when her husband fell ill and looked as if he might die.

One day, after a visit from the doctor confirmed that he had not long to live, Mabel had to go shopping. "Harold," she said. "I won't be gone long. I has to get some flour and some raisins. But if you feels like dying afore I comes back, mind to blow out the candle first."

Harold was still alive when his wife came back, and indeed it appeared that he might recover, for there was a bit of colour in his cheeks. Mabel tucked him up nice and cosy in his bed, wiped his nose, straightened his night-cap, and then went into the back kitchen to get on with her daily tasks. Soon the unmistakable smell of Welsh cakes on the griddle wafted into the bedroom, and Harold was greatly moved. "Mabel bach," he cried. "I smell fresh Welsh cakes on the stove! I think I could manage one or two!"

"Hush now, husband," came the reply. "You'll manage nothing of the kind, for those are for the funeral!"

## Nice Day for a Trip

Vince Evans from Cardigan was making his first trip by plane, and was on his way from Heathrow to San Francisco on a Boeing 747. About half-way through the 13-hour flight, and 50,000 feet above the icy wastes of Greenland, Vince was greatly surprised to see Will Thomas from Gwbert coming along the aisle towards him from the non-smokers end of the plane. "Good Lord," said Vince in a loud voice. "Fancy seein' you up here, Will!"

"Good morning, Vince," replied Will, equally surprised. "I thought you would be at Cardigan mart today."

"No no, I'm havin' a bit of a trip to visit my Cousin Wilma. What a nice summers day it is up here, to be sure. An' have you just got on?"

## After Due Consideration

Gwynfor Pantglas was an old farmer who lived in the wild and beautiful hills near Ystrad Meurig. He was hardly ever seen in the village, but one day he popped in to the village post office and asked for a stamp. "What price would you like, Gwynfor bach?" asked the post mistress.

"Well now, that would be hard to say," replied the old farmer. "Please to show me what you can offer."

Raising her eyes to heaven, and wondering when last Gwynfor had come down from the hills, the post mistress took out several sheets of stamps of different denominations and showed them to the old man. He spent a long time examining them minutely, and asked numerous questions concerning their prices, colours, sizes and so forth. The post mistress was beginning to get exasperated when the old man suddenly came to a decision. Pointing to a large unbroken sheet of a hundred halfpenny stamps, he pointed to one right in the middle and enquired as to its price. "Why, it costs a halfpenny, just like all the others," explained the good lady.

"Duw Duw," said Gwynfor. "That is a very reasonable price indeed for such a pretty stamp. Please to give me that one there, for I likes it better than all the others. After due consideration I do declare it gives much better value for money than them that is on the edges."

## Not Actually Needed

Once upon a time a Cardigan grocer was behind his counter when a very scruffy little boy came in, looking somewhat ill at ease. The grocer had never seen him before. "What can I do for you, young man?" he asked. "Please sir, my mam says please to sell me a roll of toilet paper."

The grocer took down a roll from the shelf and said "That will be threepence, please." The boy paid over the money, took the toilet roll and scuttled out of the shop.

First thing on Monday morning the little boy was back again, carrying the toilet roll under his arm and carrying a letter in his hand. "Please sir," he explained, "my mam says please to read the letter." The grocer opened it up and read as follows:

*"Dear Sir, Billy is taking the roll of toilet paper back to you, and please to pay him the money back what he paid you. We will not be needing the toilet roll. Our visitors never came."*

## Not So Urgent

Early one morning Dr Jones of Cardigan was sound asleep after an all-night case when he was awakened by the incessant ringing of his telephone. He dragged himself wearily to the phone and picked up the receiver. "Doctor, Doctor," said a female voice at the other end, "this is Thomas Brynawelon. Please come at once! A matter of life and death it is!" And with that the line went dead. The good doctor dressed hurriedly and rushed out of the house.

When he arrived at Brynawelon he found that the caller and her family were all perfectly calm. "It's all right now, doctor bach," said Mrs Thomas. "You could just as well have stayed at home."

The doctor was furious. "Then why did you call me out?" he demanded.

"Well now, doctor," interjected the man of the house. "Little Billy told us he'd swallowed a half-crown, and we feared the worst. Things was looking very bad indeed. But then we realised it was only a penny piece he'd swallowed. We found the half-crown on the floor and then we felt much better."


## No Great Hurry

Ifans Pwll lived on a little farm about three miles from Tregaron with wife and extended family. One dark winter's day he came rushing into the kitchen shouting at the top of his voice. "Mabel bach," he cried, "the barn's on fire! It's full of hay and it's not insured! Quick, dial 999 and get the fire brigade!"

"Don't be daft, Ifans bach," said Mabel. "Don't you remember that you insured the barn only last week with Perkins Provincial?"

At this, Mr Ifans uttered a great sigh of relief. "So I did, Mabel, now you comes to remind me," he said. "Never mind about the phone call. But we has to get a message to the fire station — I'll get out the water buckets and you send Grandma very urgent on her bike!"


## Only Just Passed

Reverend Geraint Hughes was a vicar in a well-known Cardi town. Unfortunately he fell ill and had to go to hospital for an operation. After a few days he was visited by the churchwarden, who said on his arrival at the bedside: "Vicar, there's nice it is to see you looking so healthy. We had a meeting of the Parochial Church Council last night, and I am pleased to tell you that a resolution wishing you a speedy recovery was passed by fourteen votes to twelve."

## Trouble with the Dog

A good-hearted Cardigan lady was collecting for Christian Aid, and left envelopes with about fifty householders for later collection. When she called back at one house on North Road the lady who opened the door said: "Very sorry I am, but I can't give you anything because the dog have ate the envelope." The collector was not at all put out by this, and replied "Don't you worry, Mrs Evans. I have a spare envelope with me."

"There wouldn't be no point in me having it, bach," said Mrs Evans. "Sure as eggs the dog will eat that one too."

## No Great Worries

Mrs Maggie Williams of Llandysul was celebrating her 105th birthday. She was visited by the reporter from the "Tivyside Advertiser" who asked her lots of questions about her childhood memories, her marriage and her family. At last she was asked whether at her great age she had any worries, and she immediately replied: "No no, bach. Not any longer I don't, not since I managed to get my youngest son Brynmor into the Old People's Home."

## Cardi Insurance Policy

There was once an insurance company based in Cardigan. Naturally enough, it had a great reputation for being very cautious when it came to paying out on insurance claims.

One day Gethin Mathias met a very angry bull in a field, which resulted in him being tossed over the hedge and breaking his arm. In due course he put in a claim for £20 compensation to the insurance company, and was none too pleased when he received this reply:

*"Dear Mr Mathias,*

*We are sorry to say that we are unable to entertain your claim for compensation following your unfortunate encounter with the bull. You claim that it was an accident, but having considered all the circumstances very carefully we have come to the conclusion that the bull threw you over the hedge **quite deliberately.** We therefore conclude that the incident was not covered by your policy. If, however, you would like us to arrange cover for future deliberate acts of violence against your person we will be only too delighted to give you a quotation.        Yours etc,*

*Jimmy Jones  (Manager)*

## Good Value for Money

Cardis are renowned for obtaining good value for money, and also for their accurate knowledge of human nature. One dark winter's evening a Cardi was travelling by taxi to Aberystwyth from his home near Tregaron. As the vehicle came into the outskirts of the town he realised that he had left his wallet and all his money at home.

So he leaned forward towards the taxi driver and said: "Can you just stop at the next garage, please, so that I can get a box of matches? I have dropped a £50 note somewhere in the back of the car, and until I can light a match it's too dark to find it."

The taxi driver duly stopped at the next garage. The Cardi passenger got out and went into the shop. When he came out, the taxi had disappeared, and he completed the last hundred yards of his journey on foot with a happy smile on his face.

## How to Cope with Disaster

An English tourist was doing some shopping in Cardigan, and when he returned to his posh car in the car-park he found a great dent in its side. He was furious, but then he noticed a note stuck under one of the windscreen wipers, and was cheered up to some extent by the thought that the guilty person was intent on putting right the damage he had inflicted. Taking the note, he read as follows:

"Dear Sir, The people who saw me reverse my car into the side of your car are now watching me write this note. They are doubtless quite convinced that I am writing down my name and address so that you can send me the bill for the damage. Ho! Ho! Do they think I'm stupid? Best wishes from a mysterious friend."

## Threatening Behaviour

Two good friends, one from Aberdeen and the other from Cardigan, were in Cardigan post office queuing for their Christmas stamps. Suddenly an armed man rushed in with a balaclava helmet over his head and shouted: "This is a hold-up! You lot in the queue — give me all the money you have in your wallets and hand-bags!"

Quick as a flash, the Cardi friend took all the money from his wallet and handed it to the man from Aberdeen. "Here you are, Angus," he whispered. "This is the twenty-five quid I borrowed from you three years ago!"

# Getting Off Lightly

A Cardiganshire man went for a drive down to Tenby, and on the approach road to the town he was stopped for speeding by a traffic policeman in a panda car.
"Name please?" said the policeman.

"Iorwerth ap Rhydderch ap Cadwaladr ap Arnallt ap Llwyd"

"Place of residence?"

"Bwlchgwynt, Gwernddwr, Llanfihangel y Creuddyn."

"Well, don't let me catch you speeding again."


# Hardly Worth It

Tomos Tomos of Cardigan was feeling benevolent, and one day he met William Williams of Fishguard in a local pub. "Good evening to you, Mr Williams bach," he said. "I have just remembered that I borrowed half a crown from you fifteen years ago. Now then, let me repay my debt."

"Don't you bother, Mr Tomos bach," replied William. "After all this time I hardly think it's worth changing my opinion of you just for half a crown."

# Most Unusual

A Cardigan horse dealer was spotted in the High Street by a recent customer. "You filthy crook." shouted the angry customer. "You know that horse you sold me last week?"

"Yes, I remember it well," replied the dealer. "What about it?"

"He fell over yesterday, dead as a duck, and left me feeling sick as a parrot."

"Well I never!" said the dealer. "I told you when I sold him to you that he had some funny little ways with him, but I do declare I never knew him to do that before."

## Always Ahead

The redoubtable local newspaper called the "Tivyside Advertiser" once carried an announcement of the death of Councillor William Jones of Pentood. Unfortunately it later turned out that the said William Jones was not dead. The following week the paper printed this correction:

*"Last week we were the first newspaper to announce the death of Cllr William Jones of Pentood. Today we are the first newspaper to deny the report. The "Tivyside" is always in the lead."*

## Careful with the Cash

An old lady from Tregaron, who happened to be rather deaf, went into the old-fashioned draper's shop in the town centre. "And what would be the price of this silk, if you please?" she inquired of the young shop assistant.

"Seven shillings a yard," came the reply.

"Seventeen shillings indeed!" exclaimed the old lady. "Careful with the cash I am. Thirteen shillings a yard is absolutely the most that I will offer you."

"Only **seven** shillings, madam, is the price of the silk."

"Oh, seven shillings did you say?" came the rejoinder. "Well then, I'll give you not a penny more than five bob!"

## Quite Satisfactory Indeed

A disgruntled customer went into a well-known Cardigan jeweller to return a brooch he had purchased the day before. "I bought this yesterday," said the customer, "and I am not at all happy with the quality of it now that I have had a chance to examine it carefully."

"There's sorry I am to hear it, sir."

"Well, you told me that you would return my money to me if it was not entirely satisfactory."

"Quite right you are, sir," said the jeweller. "But it was quite satisfactory indeed. In fact, I never handled better money in my life."


## Same Old Stuff

An old spinster from Cardigan decided she had better move with the times, so she rented a television set. Unfortunately she found it difficult to come to terms with many of the things she saw on the flickering screen. At last she sent the TV set back to the shop, complaining that she disapproved of the programmes being shown.

Next day she went out and bought a goldfish bowl and two goldfish instead. At first she found it most restful watching the fish in the glass bowl. But after a few days she returned them to the pet-shop. "Same old rubbish," she said to the shop-keeper. "Nothing but sex and violence."


## Perfectly Reasonable

Councillor Gwynfor Griffiths of New Quay walked out of the Planning Committee meeting of Ceredigion District Council and was accosted by a detective. "Are you Councillor Griffiths?" he asked.

"Yes indeed. And what can I do for you, officer?"

"Did you vote just now in favour of a planning permission for a new bungalow for Mathias Tygwyn?"

"Yes indeed I did. A most splendid bungalow it will be, for sure."

"Well, we have evidence that you have accepted a £50 bribe from Mr Mathias, and that is a criminal offence."

"No no, officer. You has got it all wrong. I voted for Mr Mathias to have his bungalow because I happens to like him."

"Well, there we have you, Councillor. We have concrete evidence from the bank that you accepted £50 from the applicant."

"Nothing wrong with that, officer. It is plain common sense, indeed, that if somebody gives you £50 you are going to like him."

## Not Worth the Effort

Once upon a time, back in the bad old days when all the princes of Dyfed were fighting against each other, Prince Rhys ap Rhys of Ceredigion was having a feud with Prince Gruffydd ap Gruffydd of Dinefwr. Rhys and his henchmen went off on a raid, and disguised as poor peasants they stole Gruffydd's heavy wooden throne. They carted it back towards Cardigan, but before they could reach home they were overtaken by darkness. They took shelter in a grass hut belonging to a peasant, and hid the throne in the rafters. Then they spent the evening eating, drinking and making merry. At the height of the revelry the rafters of the flimsy grass hut collapsed, and the throne fell on top of Prince Rhys, killing him instantly. The moral of this tale is that people who live in grass houses shouldn't stow thrones.

## Worth Every Penny

An antique dealer from up England way was roaming around the Tregaron area looking for antiques. Passing along a narrow lane, he came across a very old man chopping sticks on the front doorstep of his cottage. "My goodness, dear sir," said the antiques dealer. "That looks like a very old axe you have there."

"Indeed it is," said the old man. "It once belonged to Owain Glyndwr, the great Prince of Wales, and you can have it for £5000."

"Good Lord!" exclaimed the dealer. "That makes it about 600 years old! It has certainly stood up well over all those years."

"Indeed it have," replied the peasant. "In our family we looks after things very well. This here axe is in such good condition on account that it have had five new handles and six new heads since Prince Owain gave it to us."

## Quite Enough of You

An English tourist was wandering around in the hill country around Llywernog, where there are lots of old lead mines. Suddenly he heard a voice calling for help from a deep hole in the ground. He went up to the edge of the deep hole and looked down, but it was so deep and so dark that he could see nothing. "Help! Help!" shouted the voice.

"Hello down there!" shouted the Englishman. "Have you had an accident?"

"Daro, there's lucky I am that somebody have come by. Fell in, I did, when I was out fetchin' the sheep, and I have had a nasty pull on the old leg."

"Who is it that's down there?" called the stranger.

"Iestyn ap Gwilym ap Sion ap Rhys."

"Well, if there's that many of you down there you can jolly well help each other out!" said the Englishman, and went on his way.

## Conversation in Llangranog

Bethan and Megan met at the Post Office on a Friday morning when they were collecting their allowances.

"Morning Megan," said Bethan. "There's weather we are having. And the price of things! I was hopin' for a bit of fish for dinner today, but the cost in Siop Popeth have gone beyond. Are you keepin' well?"

"Not too bad, thank you, bach. But off sick I am, these last few days, with the old back. But grateful I am that I'm not so bad as Ellen Glan-y-mor, poor dab."

"Yes indeed. Most likely her troubles have come on since she buried her husband. It must be nearly a twelvemonth now. Is she still under the doctor with her waterworks?"

"No no, bach. I do hear she have now gone under the specialist at Bronglais."

"Ooh, there's posh for you!"

## Well Organized

An old Cardi gentleman was out for a walk with his little grandson, and they took a short cut through the local cemetery. Pausing before a gravestone, the old man said "Now then, Elfed, there lies a very honest man. He died owing me £50, but during his life he always struggled to pay off his debts. If anybody has gone to heaven, he has."

The walked on a bit further, and the grandfather stopped at another grave. Pointing at the headstone, he said "Now there's a different type of man altogether. John Jenkins owed me £40 and he died without ever trying to pay me back. If anybody has gone to hell, he has."

The little boy thought for a while, and then piped up "You know, grandpa, you are very lucky indeed."

"Oh, and why should that be?" asked the old man.

"Well, whichever place you end up in, you'll have a tidy few quid to draw on."


## Can't Afford it

A Cardigan housewife was looking around the Electricity Board showroom when a salesman came up to her and attempted to sell her a home freezer that was on a special offer. "After all, madam," he said, "if you buy it at this price you will undoubtedly save more than enough on your food bills to pay for it."

"Well, there's nice for you," replied the housewife. "A tidy freezer it is, for sure, but I has to tell you that we are buying a car on the bus fares we save, paying for the washing machine with the money we don't spend at the launderette, and paying for the house on the rent we save. Sad to say, my hubby have worked it out that we just can't afford to save no more just now."


## Not Too Bad Considering

The projectionist of the Theatr Mwldan Film Society in Cardigan lived on a smallholding just outside the town. One day two of his goats found a can full of film in the yard which had fallen out of the boot of his clapped-out car. One of them nuzzled it until the lid fell off, and for a while the two of them pushed the spool around in the yard. The film came loose, and the first goat ate a few frames of it. She liked the taste of it, and so the second goat took a few mouthfuls also. They tucked in with relish, and soon the whole film had been eaten up. Licking her lips, the first goat said "Best film in ages. Wasn't that great?" "Oh I don't know," replied the second goat. "I thought the book was better."

# The Cost of Marriage

A newly married farmer from Lampeter was having a few pints in the local pub having sold twenty calves at the mart. "Marriage is all very well," he said. "But my wife is always asking me for money. Last week she wanted £100. The week before she asked me for £250. Yesterday she wanted £25, and I'll be damned if she didn't ask me for £50 before I went to the mart this morning!"

"Jawch! That don't sound too good," said his friend. "What on earth do she want all that money for?"

"Goodness knows," replied the young farmer. "I've never found out, since I never gives her any!"

# All in the Mind

A new Christian Science church opened up in Aberystwyth, and quickly attracted a sizeable congregation. One day the pastor met one of his congregation in the street. "Good morning, Mrs Edwards," he said. "And how is your husband today?"

"Not too good, thank you, reverend," came the reply. "The doctor have been, and says he is very ill with the flu."

"No no," corrected the pastor. "Such things are all in the mind. The Lord will protect his flock. You should simply say that you husband is *under the impression* that he is very ill."

The woman nodded meekly and replied "Grateful I am for your help, reverend. I'll remember that in future."

A few weeks later the pastor met the woman in the street again. "And how is your husband getting on these days?" he asked.

"Well, reverend," she replied. "Since last Thursday he's been under the impression that he's dead."

# A Helping Hand

A Baptist minister was driving along a country lane near Ffostrasol in his Morris Minor when a large black Mercedes careered around the bend, spun out of control, and crashed into him. Both cars ended up in the ditch severely damaged.

Luckily neither driver was injured. The driver of the Mercedes, who was a wealthy Cardi farmer, climbed out of the wreck and staggered over towards the minister.

"Good Heavens!" exclaimed the minister. "That was very close indeed. You could have killed me!"

"I'm very sorry indeed," replied the farmer, taking a flask of whisky from his pocket. "Here, have a swig of this. It will help to calm your nerves."

"I don't normally indulge," said the minister, "But I am very shaken up, and I appreciate your kind gesture." And with that he took a generous swig from the flask. Feeling somewhat calmer, he handed the flask back to the farmer. "Here you are," he said. "Have a swig yourself."

"Oh no, reverend," replied the Cardi calmly. "I never drink after an accident. But I've called the police on my mobile phone, and I'll just wait here quietly with you until they arrive."


## Very Nasty Incident

Thomas Self Raising was a Tregaron baker, so named because his wife was very straight-laced and reputedly frigid. One day he was delivering the bread to an isolated farm near the town when he was attacked by a vicious gander. The creature chased him down the lane, got him into a corner, and bit him in a place that cannot be mentioned for reasons of delicacy. After examining the damage the poor fellow drove with difficulty into town and called in at the nearest pub for a stiff drink. He told his tale of woe to the landlord, who gave him a free brandy, roared with laughter, and said "Now then, Thomas bach, they do say in China that it is the early bird that catches the worm."

By lunch-time poor Thomas was suffering from considerable pain and swelling, and he called in at the surgery for treatment. After examining him the doctor said he had seen nothing like it in forty years of general practice. He gave him a prescription for some antiseptic ointment, and told him to keep the affected part nice and warm until the pain had eased off. His wife, very embarrassed, called at the chemist for the ointment, and after that nobody saw Thomas Self Raising for a week.

Then Mrs Thomas turned up at the surgery again. The other patients were surprised to see that she had a sparkle in her eye and a flush upon her cheek. When her turn came she went into the consulting room. "Please to have some more of that wonderful ointment, doctor bach," she said. "I have been treating the patient according to the instructions. He do still complain about the pain, but by God the ointment is having a most wonderful effect upon the swelling!"

# Kind Deed in Capel Cynon

An old farmer from Capel Cynon had a valuable Border Collie named Bess, with whom he had won various prestigious sheepdog trials. Unfortunately, whenever she was on heat there was an influx of dogs of all shapes and sizes from neighbouring farms, and the farmer discovered that the only way to keep them away was to give her hindquarters a good soaking with petrol.

One day he was pouring petrol over Bess's backside when his little grandson came into the yard and asked what he was doing. Somewhat embarrassed, the farmer mumbled something to the effect that she needed the petrol so that she could carry on working on the farm without interference from other dogs. The little boy appeared perfectly satisfied with the explanation and went back to playing with his toys.

Next day the farmer was sitting at his desk in the living room when his grandson came rushing in. "Come quick, grandpa!" exclaimed the child. "It's Bess — run out of petrol, she has!"

"What do you mean, run out of petrol?" asked the old farmer.

"Well," said the boy, "that big old dog from up the road is standing behind her giving her a push down the hill. There's kind he is, trying very hard to get her started."

# THEY DO SAY ........

** that you can tell the good Baptist people of Ceredigion from those who have not been saved. The Baptists are the ones who take the swings out of their budgies' cages on Sundays in case they enjoy themselves.

** that a Cardi is defined as a Scotsman robbed of his generosity.

** that a Cardiganshire farmer once included in his will the words "I leave to my good wife Marged all the goods in the bed, over the bed and under the bed."

** that a Cardi farmer once stuck a mirror to his dog's feeding bowl to make him think he was getting two bones for his dinner.

** that a genuine Cardi can buy something from a Jew and sell it to a Scotsman, and still make a tidy profit.

** that an old Cardi proverb says "There is one advantage in being poor — it's very inexpensive."

** that a Cardi farmer had an exceptionally heavy crop of potatoes on his land one year. He complained to a neighbour "Duw Duw, this is a bad business, Dai. Such a crop have placed a terrible strain on the land, and no good will come of it."

** that another Cardi proverb says "You can't take it with you when you go — and even if you can it will melt when you get there."

** that in a well-known Cardigan bakery they make the bread so light in texture that a pound loaf only weighs eight ounces.

** that a Cardi dairyman was so mean that after skimming the cream off the top of his milk he would turn it upside down and skim the cream off the bottom as well.

** that centuries of careful breeding have resulted in Cardis having long pockets and short arms.

** that according to tradition the true Cardi removes his cap only on entering the chapel and the bank, and bows only to God and his sovereign.

** that while Pembrokeshire men buy TV sets and sit watching them, Cardiganshire men buy wall safes instead and watch them for four hours every evening.

** that eighty percent of farmers living north of Aberaeron take the "Cambrian News". The other twenty percent pay for it.